SCHOLASTIC ★ AT-HOME ★ PHONICS READING PROGRAM

Ants to Zebras: Silly Animal Jokes and Riddles

by Nancy Leber
Illustrated by Tony Griego

SCHOLASTIC INC.
New York Toronto London Auckland Sydney Mexico City New Delhi Hong Kong

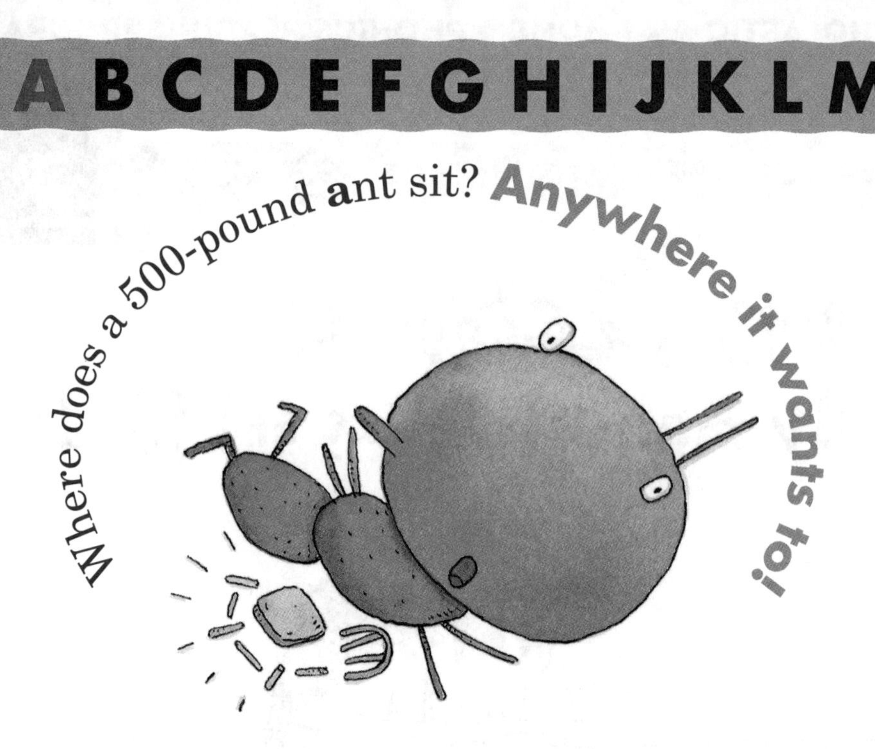

What do ants have that no other animals have?

Cute little baby ants.

Who would marry a monkey's uncle?

A monkey's aunt.

What is the biggest ant in the whole world?

A giant!

What ant is huge and gray? An elephant.

What did the **b**ird say when its new cage broke?

Who do birds marry?

They marry their tweet-hearts!

What would you get if you crossed a bird and a frog?

A frog that leaps and peeps.

Which TV show do most **c**ows watch after dinner?

The Nightly Moos.

How do you know when a cow has a cold?

It sneezes,

What do you call cows that sit on grass all day?

Ground beef.

Why did those chickens run away from home?

Because they were sick of being cooped up.

When is it bad luck to have
a black cat behind you?

What happened to the mother-to-be cat
who ate a whole ball of wool?

Its kittens were all born with mittens!

Where does a 500-pound **d**uck sit?

Anywhere it wants to!

What do ducks like to watch on TV?
Duck-umentaries.

What is a fast duck?
A quick quack.

What goes tick-tock, bow-wow?
A watch dog.

Where do dogs park their cars?
In barking lots!

What do you do when your dog eats the whole newspaper?
Take the words right out of its mouth!

What treat does a dog like on a hot day?
An ice cream bone.

When is an **e**lephant light?

How would you get five elephants in a car?

Put two in the front seat, two in the back, and one in the trunk.

How would you get four hippos in a car?
You can't — it's full of elephants.

What happens when you cross an elephant and a telephone?

Where does a 500-pound eagle sit?
Anywhere it wants to!

Which **f**ish is the brightest?

A starfish.

How do you know fish are smart? They live in schools.

Which is faster: a hot fish or a cold one?
A hot fish is faster because you can catch a cold.

What is the best way to catch a fish?

Ask someone to *throw* it to you!

Where on the globe might you find a **g**orilla?

You wouldn't! A gorilla is much bigger than a globe!

Where does a 500-pound gorilla sit?

Anywhere it wants to!

How can you tell if there is a **h**ippo in the bathtub?

The tub is full, and water is all over the place!

What do you get if you cross an **i**guana and a frog?

A leaping lizard.

When is a **j**aguar nice to a mouse?

When the jaguar wants a light bite.

Why is it hard to make **k**angaroos cry? **They are always so hoppy.**

Rose had 12 **l**ambs. All but nine ran away from home. How many lambs did Rose have left?

How does a llama get up in the morning?
It sets an a-llama clock.

Who has more fun when you tickle a **m**ule — you or the mule?

The mule may like it, but you'll get a bigger kick out of it.

What kind of animal needs oil?

Mice. They squeak.

What is the biggest mouse in the world?

A hippopota-mouse.

Who takes care of sick fish?

Nurse sharks.

Where does a 500-pound **o**tter sit? **Anywhere it wants to!**

A **p**ig wrote a note to a pal.
What did the pig use to write with?

A pigpen.

Why did the three little pigs run all the way home?

They were hamsick.

What did the pig use when it burned its nose?

Oinkment

What do you call a **q**uail sitting under a big umbrella, wearing a big hat, and sunglasses?

A pale quail.

What does a **r**abbit use to keep its fur neat?

What do you call a rabbit who plans to run away from home?

Hare today, gone tomorrow.

How do you stop a **s**kunk from smelling?
Hold its nose.

How did the sick sheep get to the hospital?
It rode in a l-ambulance.

What do you call a well-dressed **t**urtle?
A dapper snapper!

If farmers could grow animals,
what would they grow?
Uni-corns.

How do you make a **w**alrus float?
Put it in a glass of soda with two scoops of ice cream.

What do you get when two o**x**en bump into each other?

Which animal talks a lot?

A **y**ak.

What do you get if you cross a turtle and a yak?

A snappy talker.

The ABCs go from A to Z.
What goes from Z to A?

Zebra!

Phonics Reader 42 ★ Words to Sound Out

long o with final e	long u with final e
bone	cute
broke	huge
globe	mule
hole	use
home	
jokes	
lone	
nose	
note	
Rose	
telephone	
those	
whole	
wrote	

Phonics Reader 42 ★ Words to Remember

elephant kangaroo which zebra

Phonics Reader 42 ★ Story Words

iguana jaguar